Walking with Jesus

Walking with Jesus

Stories About Real People Who Return Good for Evil

Mary Clemens Meyer

Illustrated by Harriet Miller

HERALD PRESS
Scottdale, Pennsylvania
Waterloo, Ontario

Library of Congress Cataloging-in-Publication Data
Meyer, Mary Clemens, 1954-
  Walking with Jesus : stories about real people who return good for evil / Mary
Clemens Meyer ; illustrated by Harriet Miller.
    p.   cm.
  ISBN 0-8361-3574-1 (alk. paper)
  1. Peace—Religious aspects—Christianity—Case studies—Juvenile literature.
2. Love—Religious aspects—Christianity—Case studies—Juvenile literature. I. Title.
BT736.4.M48   1992
241'.697—dc20   92-10912
                                                                                         CIP

The paper used in this publication meets the minimum requirements of American
National Standard for Information Sciences—Permanence of Paper for Printed
Library Materials, ANSI Z39.48-1984.

The stories in this book originally appeared in the children's publication, *Story
Friends*.

WALKING WITH JESUS
Copyright © 1992 by Herald Press, Scottdale, Pa. 15683
  Published simultaneously in Canada by Herald Press,
  Waterloo, Ont. N2L 6H7. All rights reserved.
Library of Congress Catalog Number: 92-10912
International Standard Book Number: 0-8361-3574-1
Printed in the United States of America
Design by Merrill R. Miller/Art by Harriet Miller

1 2 3 4 5 6 7 8 9 10 98 97 96 95 94 93 92

To my children
Susanna, Christopher, and Katie—
growing peacemakers.

Contents

Grandpa, Brave Man

Mary was excited. This morning she and her younger brother had wakened early to come across the fields with Mama to Grandpa Albrecht's farm. Mama was driving into town with Grandpa today, and the children would stay at the farm.

Sometimes Mary and Lawrence got to ride in Grandpa's shiny car, too. They loved to hear the loud "A-ooo-ga!" sound the horn made when they squeezed its rubber bulb. Not many people had cars in 1919, and it was a special treat to ride in one.

But Mary thought it was great fun just to visit Grandpa's farm. Grandpa's orchard and garden provided heaping baskets of fruits and vegetables all summer and fall, and the busy beehives in the orchard were full of honey. Whenever they visited Grandpa's farm, Mary and Lawrence ate thick slices of homemade bread, spread with lots of freshly churned butter and golden honey.

The best thing about the farm, though, was Grandpa himself. Mary loved to be around him. He was a big, strong man, but gentle and kind. He helped people who needed food and money. On Sundays Grandpa sat up on the bench behind the pulpit at Willow Springs Church, and sometimes he preached the sermon.

Now Mary could hardly wait to start her day on the farm. The trees in the orchard were hanging heavy with apples, and the housekeeper was sure to serve apple pie with whipped cream for dessert.

Mama and Grandpa were almost ready to leave. Mama was untying her apron after helping with the breakfast dishes, and Grandpa was tidying his desk. Mary was waiting to wave good-by to them before running out to the orchard for a crisp, sweet apple.

Suddenly they heard angry shouts from outside the front door. Grandpa strode through the dining room to open the door. The women gathered in the kitchen doorway.

Mary hid behind her mother.

There were two men outside, but they didn't come up to the door. Their faces were red and angry. They kept shouting at Grandpa.

What is wrong? Why are they mad at Grandpa? Mary wondered, with tears in her eyes.

The men yelled angry words she didn't understand—"yellow, CO camp, tar and feather."

"We'll come back with the others to tar and feather you," they shouted. "We'll get the other Mennonite preacher, too!"

Mary looked at Grandpa—her big, kind grandpa. He stood calmly, rubbing his arm with his great big hand as he often did. He answered the men quietly and in a friendly tone. He didn't seem afraid.

Finally the men walked away. The women stared after them with worried faces. Mary let go of Mama's skirt and asked, "Mama, what does 'tar and feather' mean?"

Mama took Mary's hand and sat down tiredly on a chair. "Mary," she said, "when they tar and feather a man, they take off his clothes. Then they paint him all over with sticky black pitch, like they use on rooftops. They press feathers all over him and parade around with him to make him feel ashamed."

"But why, Mama?" Mary pleaded. "Why would they want to do that to Grandpa?"

"Mary, these men think Grandpa should be ashamed that his son didn't join the army and go to fight in the war. You remember when Uncle Julius went away to work in a special camp, don't you?"

Mary nodded, and Mama went on. "He went to work there instead of going to fight in the war, because Jesus said God loves all people. Your uncle doesn't want to kill anyone. I guess those men just can't understand that. They think Grandpa and Uncle Julius are 'yellow'—afraid to fight. That's why they are so angry."

Mary knew Grandpa wouldn't be afraid of anything. He was always so calm and sure of himself. But she was afraid for him. She noticed him now, standing quietly nearby.

"Grandpa," she asked, turning her small, scared face up to his big, kindly one, "Will they really come to tar and feather you?"

"No, Mary," he said with a gentle smile. "I don't believe they will."

And Grandpa was right. They never did come.

Mary Kaufmann always remembered what she saw and heard that day in Tiskilwa, Illinois. When Mary grew up, she became the wife of a preacher. Her youngest son was called to fight in a war, but he chose to help people in a hospital instead.

Mama's Example

It was a bright summer Sunday at the Aurora Mennonite Church in Ohio. In the primary classroom, Mary Yoder's teacher was finishing the Sunday school lesson.

"Jesus helped Peter's sick mother-in-law by making her well," she said. "Can you think of someone you know who helps others like Jesus did?"

The class was silent for a moment, then several children began talking at once.

"One at a time, please," said Mrs. Miller. "John, you may go first."

13

Mary sat quietly and listened as her classmates talked. She knew what she would say when her turn came.

At last Mrs. Miller called on her. "Mary, who do you know who helps like Jesus did?"

"My mama," said Mary, promptly. "She's the kindest person I know."

"Can you tell us about a time when your mother helped someone?" asked Mrs. Miller.

"Last summer we got some new neighbors—the Harshbargers," answered Mary. "They just moved up from the South, and Mama took my sister Martha and me along to visit them. They had five children, and they were really poor.

"Well, while we were there, Mama saw their two big apple trees, full of apples. She asked the mother if she was going to can applesauce. But Mrs. Harshbarger said she didn't know how. So we went back the next day, and Mama showed her. We made so much applesauce it took two days to get it all done!"

"That's being kind like Jesus," said Mrs. Miller. "Did your mother visit the family again?"

"Oh, yes!" said Mary. "Mama showed Mrs. Harshbarger how to brown the flour when she made gravy, 'cause they had lots of meals with just potatoes and flour gravy. And she helped with big dinners when the threshers came.

"And when the Harshbargers had a baby, Mama went to help. Last month, on Mama's birthday, the Harshbargers gave her a real nice Bible. It even has her name, Esther Yoder, printed on the cover in gold!"

Suddenly Mary realized how much she was talking. She stopped, embarrassed. The other children were all looking at her.

But Mrs. Miller smiled. "That's a good example of helping, Mary," she said. "We can learn a lot about being kind from your mother."

Mary's face glowed with happiness. She was proud of Mama.

"Now, class," Mrs. Miller went on, "this week I would like each of you to show kindness to someone you think especially needs a friend. It might be someone you know, or someone you don't know at all. Then next Sunday we'll share what happened."

The hallway buzzed with excitement as the children left the classroom. Whom would they find to help this week?

Mary thought about it all the way home in the back seat of the car. She watched Mama's gentle face as she talked to Papa in the front. Could she learn to be kind like her mother?

A few days later a worn-out, dusty car came rattling up the Yoders' drive. It was the peddler from Cleveland. Mary had always been scared of him, because he was dirty and smelly and talked in a funny way.

She started to run away and hide, but then she remembered her Sunday school assignment. Mrs. Miller wanted her to be kind to someone who needed a friend this week.

Mary turned and hurried into the house to tell Mama the peddler was there. Mama walked out to greet him as he hobbled up the walk in his ragged, dark clothes.

"Hello," said Mama, warmly, holding out her hand. "It's good to see you again."

The peddler smiled. Mary shrank behind Mama at the sight of his dirty gap teeth.

"You must be hungry," Mama went on. "We've already finished our lunch, but I'll have something ready for you in no time. Please, come in."

The peddler happily followed them into the house.

Mary helped Mama in the kitchen all she could, but she stayed out of the dining room where the peddler sat. She knew she should talk to him and be friendly like Jesus would, but it was so hard! How did Mama do it?

Slurp, slurp. The peddler was eating noisily. Mary peered around the kitchen door and watched. He had arranged the red ripe tomato slices in a ring around the edge of his plate and was eating them one by one.

Mary began to feel sorry for him. He looked so old and tired sitting there. She knew he had no home, and that he lived in his car. She wanted him to know she was his friend.

Just then Mama touched her shoulder with a plate of fragrant, homemade bread. "Mary," she asked, "will you please serve the bread to our guest?"

Slowly Mary walked to the table and held out the plate to the peddler. He turned his head and looked up at her.

Suddenly Mary didn't feel afraid anymore. "Would you like some bread?" she asked politely. Then she looked straight into the peddler's eyes and gave him a big, friendly smile.

Esther Yoder never said to her children, "Be kind to strangers." She just did it. The peddler especially liked to stay at Esther's house, because she gave him a bed in the spare room instead of in the barn. When he left he would give the family fruit from his car "store." Mary always remembered that her first taste of grapefruit came from the peddler.

Neighbor Al

It was a warm, late summer afternoon. The birds were singing and hopping about on the lawn. A gentle breeze cooled Al Wengerd's face as he crossed the street to his garden. He took a deep breath of fresh air and smiled.

Al loved to come home from a long day of work, change into comfortable clothes, and walk in his garden. Seeing the straight green rows of

17

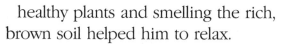

healthy plants and smelling the rich, brown soil helped him to relax.

But today an unhappy surprise was waiting for Al. He stopped at the edge of the garden and stared. Half his carrots had been pulled out and scattered on the ground. Four tomato stalks were uprooted, too, and some green beans. The plants weren't even wilted yet.

Al looked up and down the alley. No one was in sight. Angrily he stomped around his garden. *Who could have done this? And why?* he wondered. And what would he do if he knew who it was, anyway? After all, Jesus said to love your enemies, do good to those who hurt you. Al didn't feel loving right now.

The next day Al came home from work a little earlier, hoping to catch someone in his garden. Everything was fine.

But the next afternoon, Al found cabbage plants kicked open, and more tomatoes were knocked over and thrown about.

He spotted some boys down the alley playing ball. "Have you seen anyone in my garden?" he yelled.

"Oh, yeah," they answered. "Two boys, Tyrone and Matthew. They were in there a while ago. They live over there."

Al thanked the boys and walked to the black-and-white house on the corner. A woman stepped out on the porch, looking worried.

"Do you have a son named Matthew?" Al asked.

"I do."

"Well, I think he and another boy just tore up my garden."

"Yeah, we know," she replied. "We knew he got into

somebody's garden, but we didn't know whose."

Now the boy's father appeared. Al asked him to come and see the garden. The father took one look at the torn-up plants and said, "Wait here. I'll get the boys."

He soon returned with a little boy on each side. They were small and skinny—one with unruly sandy hair, the other with short, curly, black hair.

They can't be more than six years old, Al thought to himself. He had expected someone older. He felt a little less angry as he looked at the two frightened boys. They were staring at his feet.

"Did you guys do this?" Al asked. "Look at this mess! Matthew, open your eyes. Look at me. Did you do this?"

Al thought he saw them nod, but they still did not look up. He told them to follow him to the middle of the garden, but to watch the tomatoes.

Now, calm down, Al told himself. *Remember how Jesus would act.* He took a deep breath. "I planted these plants here when you were in kindergarten last spring. I watched them grow. I watered them. I pulled all the weeds. And this week I was going to pick them and put them in my refrigerator."

A sad look came into Tyrone's big, brown eyes—and into Matthew's blue eyes, peering through strands of sandy hair.

"How are we going to live in this neighborhood together?" Al went on. "You know I'm not going to steal your dad's motorcycle parked in front of his house. I know it's his, so I won't bother it. Do you think I should have to sit here on a chair all day long and protect my garden?"

The boys both said, "I'm sorry."

But Al continued, "Well, that's not quite enough. You have to make it right. You have to do something. Do either of you have any money?"

They agreed that each of the boys would pay Al fifty cents for the vegetables. They would also work in the garden one day after school when Al needed help. The boys were eager to do this and wondered if tomorrow would be okay.

"Later," Al said. "Later I'll come and get you."

The next day Matthew and his mother came to see Al. "Here's the fifty cents I owe, and here's a letter," said Matthew. Al thanked him and reminded him that they would work in the garden in a couple of weeks.

Matthew smiled. Al knelt and looked into his eyes. "We are friends," he said gently, "Thanks for coming over."

He went inside and opened the envelope Matthew had brought. He pulled out a picture the boy had drawn—tomato and pepper plants with sad faces. On the side Matthew had written, "I am sorry about the garden."

Al went to see Tyrone's parents the next day. His mother said right away that she was sorry about what Tyrone did. "He got a whoppin' from his father," she added.

She gave Tyrone fifty cents to pay for the ruined plants, and Al reminded Tyrone that he would work in the garden with him soon.

Tyrone's mother nodded her head. "The boys should work," she said. "That's fine."

On a sunny Saturday morning a few weeks later, Al went to get the boys. They acted shy but were eager to get started. The man and the two little boys pulled out all the old plants and the rest of the carrots, and they dug potatoes.

They worked hard. Tyrone and Matthew were fascinated with digging potatoes. As Al turned over the clumps of soil, they dived for anything that looked like a potato.

"Look at this big one!" they exclaimed, again and again.

By the end of the morning, all three were laughing together like old friends.

When they were finished, Al gave each boy some carrots, onions, potatoes, and a green pepper. They thanked him, grinning widely, and headed proudly down the alley for home.

Never again would Al worry about Matthew and Tyrone

wrecking his garden. Instead he could count on two pairs of friendly hands to help him next summer.

Al Wengerd was working in prison ministries in Elkhart, Indiana, when he wrote about his experience with Tyrone and Matthew in Gospel Herald *(May 19, 1987).*

Courageous Susanna

Susanna picked up baby John, rosy and smiling from his nap. She hugged him tightly to her chest, her fingers stroking his soft, baby hair. Silent tears ran down her cheeks.

"No, this can't be happening!" she told herself. "God would not let it happen!" But deep down she knew it was true. Her young husband Henry was in jail! He and a group of men had been caught trying to ride away from the war, to a place where they would not have to fight.

All of Virginia had been talking about the war for months. The Confederate army needed all the young men to fight, they said. But Henry told Susanna that he could not be a soldier. Jesus would not want him to kill.

Now Confederate soldiers had captured him and put him in the Richmond County Jail because he would not help them fight!

The next day Susanna learned that Henry had been given three choices. He could put on a uniform and fight against the Union army. He could haul supplies for the Confederate soldiers. Or he could stay in jail.

Henry chose to haul supplies. Susanna was glad; she thanked God he wasn't fighting or sitting in a damp, dirty jail.

But Henry wasn't happy. He still felt he was helping to kill people by working for the Confederate army. One day Susanna heard a noise in the house and found Henry standing in the hallway! He had left his team of horses and walked through orchards and woods to his home.

Now Henry was called a "deserter," someone who left the army without permission. Confederate soldiers would be looking for him to force him to fight.

So Henry hid in the attic of their house. Susanna took his meals up to him, and downstairs she pretended she was alone with baby John. Every time a horse came up the driveway, Susanna felt a stab of fear, thinking the soldiers were coming.

This went on for months. After some time a new baby was born to Susanna and Henry, a little girl. They named her Sarah. It was a happy time for the family, even though Henry still had to hide.

Then two-year-old Johnny became sick. Susanna did everything she could, but in a short time he died. Henry went to Johnny's funeral, but he had to act like a stranger. He couldn't get too close to his family, for soldiers were at the funeral searching for him.

After that, Henry became more restless as he hid in the attic. He began making plans to escape with other men to the North where the Confederates couldn't find them.

Finally one day Henry and sixteen other Mennonite men crossed secretly into land held by the North and made their way to Hagerstown, Maryland. Henry sent a message to Susanna, telling her to meet him there.

Susanna wanted to be with Henry, but she was afraid. *How can I get to Maryland, with a little baby, in the middle of a war?* she wondered. "Dear God," she prayed, "You helped Henry to get to Maryland. Please help me, too."

Susanna packed all she owned into a one-horse wagon, took baby Sarah, and headed for Maryland with her sister, Mrs. Rodgers. Carefully, the women drove between the two armies, the Confederates and the Union, moving north little by little.

Suddenly, Confederate soldiers appeared and grabbed Susanna's horse. She clung to the bridle, refusing to let go. But the soldiers kept working, and soon they had the horse unhitched. *I can't get to Maryland without a horse!* thought Susanna, *What will I do?* "God, please help me!" she prayed.

Just then shouts rang out among the trees. "Yanks! Yanks!" The Confederates' enemies were coming! The soldiers let go of Susanna's horse to run from the Yankees. They ordered her to follow.

"I'll do no such thing!" she answered. Susanna hitched up her horse and continued driving North.

But the long journey wasn't over. When the women reached the town of Harper's Ferry, they found the bridge burning, and there was no way to cross the river. A kind miller showed them a place where others drove across the river.

Clutching baby Sarah close to her, Susanna plunged into the

cold water and led the horse and wagon across. Her long skirts became heavy with water, and sometimes she felt her legs couldn't move another inch. But they safely reached the other side.

At last Susanna drove into Hagerstown. Relieved but very tired, she looked all around her, not knowing which way to go. "Please help me, God," she prayed. "Help me find Henry!"

As she drove slowly past a store, she glanced into the window, where a man was fixing shoes. There was something familiar about him as he bent over his work. Susanna stopped the horse and wagon to look more closely. *Why, that's Henry!* she thought, her heart beating with excitement. She could hardly believe her eyes!

Just then her husband looked up, straight at her, and she saw his eyes light up with joy. Henry rushed out of the store and caught her in his arms.

And there, on the main street of Hagerstown, Susanna and Henry laughed and talked and cried happy tears. But most of all they thanked God for bringing them together again.

Susanna Heatwole Brunk Cooprider lived from 1839 to 1909. After her Civil War adventures, she became a pioneer and raised a large family. One of her sons, George R. Brunk, became a well-known preacher. This story from Susanna's life was adapted from the book Mennonite Women *by Elaine Sommers Rich (Herald Press, 1983).*

Honest Samuel

On a golden autumn afternoon in Dayton, Virginia, Roxie Shank stopped in the orchard on her way home from school. The sun shone through the leaves of the apple trees, making speckles of light dance on the grass. Heading straight for the Golden Delicious trees, Roxie picked a large yellow apple.

Mmmm! That sweet, juicy taste was just right. Roxie stood still for a few minutes, enjoying her snack and the warm sunshine. Then suddenly she thought, "I'd better get home and help!"

APPLES FOR SALE

Helping was something Samuel and Ada Shank's children knew a lot about. With twenty-five acres of apple trees on the farm, there was always plenty to do. In spring and summer Roxie and her brothers and sisters helped spray the apple trees to kill bugs, worms, and diseases that would hurt the apples. Sometimes Papa even kept them out of school to help. In late summer and fall they helped to pick the apples, with large canvas bags strapped over their shoulders.

Then came Roxie's favorite time, when Mama made applesauce and cooked dark, spicy apple butter in the big copper kettle outside. All the children took a turn stirring.

Today when Roxie got near the house, she saw Papa grading apples out by the garage. Grading was separating the apples to sell. Smaller apples, or ones that had little scabs or bruises, were sold for only twenty-five or fifty cents a bushel. People used these for making cider. But the large, perfect apples Papa put in round or square baskets and sold for $1.00 a bushel.

He looked up now, and smiled. "Hey, there, Roxie! Your brothers and sisters went to pick up drops. Take your things in and go help."

Roxie ran in the house to obey. Pick up drops again! She wished sometime she could help grade apples instead, but that was Papa's job. He was fussy about the apples he sold.

When Roxie came back outside, she noticed a car had stopped at the garage. Someone had seen their sign, "Apples for Sale." She hung around to watch. Roxie liked to see the different people who came to buy—in cars, trucks, or even horse-drawn buggies.

This time the customers were two ladies. They were exclaiming over how beautiful the apples looked. Then Roxie heard them say to each other, "I can't believe they're this perfect all the way down through the basket."

Roxie's mouth dropped as she listened. She couldn't believe it! These women thought Papa had cheated by putting bad apples under the good ones. Papa would *never* do that!

But now the ladies turned to Papa. "May we put the apples in another container to see if they're all good?"

Roxie felt like saying, "If you think my Papa would cheat, you can go buy your apples somewhere else!"

But Papa just smiled and said, "Yes, go right ahead. Here's another basket."

Now Roxie began to be a little scared. She knew Papa would never willingly cheat. He always taught that Jesus wanted his followers to be truthful to everyone. But what if, by mistake, he had put in one apple with a bruise or a scab, or worse yet, a wormhole? What would happen then?

Roxie held her breath as she watched the two women carefully look over each apple. Finally they were done. Roxie let out a sigh of relief. Every apple was perfect!

The women happily paid for their bushel and smiled at Roxie as they walked to their car. Papa looked at her, too, and gave her a wink.

Suddenly Roxie remembered, *The drops! I'm supposed to be picking up drops!* As she ran to the orchard, she told herself that she would always try to make Jesus happy by telling the truth. Just like Papa.

Roxie learned to follow Jesus from both of her parents. Her mother, Ada, made many sandwiches for tramps that came to the door of the farmhouse. When Roxie grew up, she married a widower and became the instant mother to six children!

Maynard, Winter Friend

It was late afternoon on a cold, winter Sunday. The wind whistled outside the trailer, tossing flurries of icy snow against the windows. Inside, though, it was cozy and warm. Maynard settled himself deeper in his armchair, glad to be indoors on a day like this. His two children, Rachel and Steve, played games on the floor, while Jan, his wife, made popcorn.

Suddenly, over the sound of the wind, they heard a commotion outside. Benji, the family's little dog, was barking excitedly. Maynard jumped up from his chair and opened the door. He could see nothing wrong. Talking gently he calmed Benji.

But the moment Maynard sat down, the dog barked again.

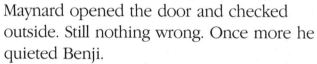

Maynard opened the door and checked outside. Still nothing wrong. Once more he quieted Benji.

But soon the dog was barking wildly. He wouldn't stop. Maynard pulled on his coat and stepped outside the door. He peered through the gathering darkness in the direction Benji was barking. All seemed well. There was their new house, as always, waiting patiently to be finished and lived in.

But wait! Maynard thought he saw something move at the back of the house. Was it only his imagination? No! There it was again, like a moving shadow, near the woodpile.

Then Maynard saw them—two small figures, their arms full of wood, darting around the corner of the house. "Why, it's a couple of boys!" he said to himself, "And they're stealing my firewood!"

Maynard started out after the boys. They were young—about eight and ten years old, he thought. Realizing someone was following them, the boys ran. One threw down his armload of wood.

Arms and legs flying, the boys tore across

the highway and up a side road to an old brick house. Maynard was close behind. The boy who had dropped his wood vanished into the dusk, but Maynard caught a glimpse of the other boy ducking into a side door.

Without stopping to think, Maynard walked up to the front door of the brick house. He knocked, and a woman opened the door. She looked tired and was wearing a coat.

She must be the boys' mother. "Did you send some boys out to get firewood?" Maynard asked. Then he told her what had happened.

The woman became furious. "I'll kill those rascals!" she yelled. "I told them to go across to the woods and pick up dead wood. They know better than to steal off somebody's woodpile."

As she talked excitedly, Maynard began to feel how cold the house was. *It must be only about forty degrees in here,* he thought.

His eyes traveled around the room. Six people, mostly children, were huddled together on a couch and chair. There was a young mother with a small baby. All were bundled in coats and blankets. A small woodstove stood in the corner, feebly burning its fuel of newspapers that the family had stuffed in.

Even with a good supply of wood, that little stove would never warm this house, Maynard knew. He said, "This stove is too small to keep your house warm. Don't you have an oil furnace?"

They did, the woman replied, but the oil had run out the night before. "The oil company won't bring us any for less than $200," she explained, "and I can't pay for that much oil right now."

Maynard thought about the big steel drum of oil sitting in his shed at home. Should he offer it to the woman? He had already let the boys keep firewood they hadn't even asked for but had stolen from him. What he really felt like doing was going home to his warm trailer and sinking into his soft armchair.

But Maynard knew that wasn't what Jesus would do, and he was a follower of Jesus. He had just gone to church that morning. Jesus would not leave a family to shiver all night in a cold house while he slept in a warm bed.

Maynard blurted out, "I have a fifty-five gallon drum of oil at home. Why don't I bring that over for you?"

The woman hesitated. "I don't have any money to pay you right now. I'll get a check in a few days."

"That's all right," Maynard said. "Just pay me when you can."

He hurried over to his shed and returned with the oil in his truck. The woman was smiling now as he lugged the big drum in.

The furnace smoked, so Maynard stayed to get it burning cleanly. As the welcome heat spread into the cold room, he not only felt warmer on the outside—he felt a special warmth on the inside, too.

Maynard Brubacher, Mount Pleasant, Pennsylvania, grew up near St. Jacobs, Ontario. He learned to be a follower of Jesus from his parents, who always treated others with love, even those who stole from them.

Nsiamindele, the Forgiver

It was a sunny, hot morning in the village of Kikaka in southern Africa. Nsiamindele, Dele (Dell-ee) for short, was only a small boy, but he had important work to do.

Early that day, before the sun was hot, he had gone to the river to fetch water for his family. Now he carried a load of sticks he had picked up for firewood. The wood was precious, because it was hard to find. And without it his mama could not cook their meals.

He handed the bundle of sticks to Mama Mavivana. She and her sister were busy grinding corn into flour. Mama's sister lived with them. She was a big help to Mama and good company, too. Dele's papa lived and worked far away in a big city. Because of his job, he could send the family enough money to buy the food and clothes they needed. But it meant they couldn't see their papa often. It was a long, long way for him to walk.

So Dele was glad that his aunt, Mama's sister, could stay with them. She was young and pretty and smiled a lot. She liked to tease Dele and play with him.

He sat and rested now, listening sleepily to the women talk as they worked. The sun was so warm. Dele yawned. He felt his eyelids closing. . . .

Suddenly he was jolted awake by the sound of angry voices. Men were grabbing Mama by the arm and taking her away. "The chief wants to see you!" they said.

With a worried look, Dele's aunt took his hand and they followed. Dele could see the bundle on his mother's back bobbing up and down as she walked. Wrapped inside the bright cloth was his tiny baby sister.

When they got to the village chief's house, the chief accused Mama of being a bad woman. Relatives had arranged for her sister to marry an old man, but her sister would not live with him. Now the chief said Mama was bad because she allowed her sister to live with her instead of forcing her to go to her husband.

The chief glared at Mama Mavivana. "What do you have to say?" he asked.

Mama replied, "I told her she should go, but she wouldn't. What can I do?" She lifted her hands helplessly.

The chief became angry. "It is your fault that your sister is not with her husband!" he shouted. He said that Mama must go to jail and do hard labor, but first she must be whipped.

Following the chief's orders, a policeman began to beat Mama. Harder and harder he hit her.

"No!" shouted Dele, "Stop!" He grabbed the policeman's legs and hung on, desperately trying to stop him. But he wasn't strong enough. The policeman kept on beating his mama until she fell to the ground.

When he finally stopped, the people who were watching rushed to help Mama. Unwrapping the bundle on her back, they found her baby daughter—beaten to death.

Dele stared in horror, his dirty face streaked with tears. His tiny sister was dead! Choking back sobs, he turned and faced the policeman.

"You killed her!" he screamed. "You killed my sister and I'll never forget. When I'm big I'll get you back for what you did to my mama and my baby sister!"

Year after year passed. In time, Nsiamindele's father and mother both died, and he went to live with one of his uncles. The uncle helped him go to a Christian school, and Dele was baptized into the church in the town of Matadi. When he finished school, he worked as a teacher, then as the manager of a railroad dining car.

One day after work one of his friends rushed to meet him. "The man who killed your sister is here in Matadi!" he said.

Dele remembered the promise he had made long ago when he was a little boy. *I swore to kill this man,* he thought. *Now I am big and strong. Now is the time to get even!*

But Dele was a Christian now. He knew it was wrong to kill for any reason. What should he do? He thought about it for hours.

Finally Dele went to one of his relatives, Don Manuel Matu, and asked him what to do.

Don Manuel said, "What did Jesus say about his enemies who nailed him to the cross?"

"He said, 'Father, forgive them, because they don't know what they are doing,' " answered Dele.

"That is the way we must forgive," said Don Manuel.

The two men read the Bible together, and Don Manuel prayed for Dele.

The next day when he was reading his Bible, Dele noticed a verse in the book of Matthew. It said, "Blessed are the merciful, for they will be shown mercy." Dele knew what he must do. He invited the policeman and Don Manuel to come to his home the next evening.

He prepared a delicious meal for his guests. When they arrived, Dele said, "In our town we say 'Don't talk to a stranger who is hungry,' so let's not talk until we have eaten."

When the men were finished with their meal, the policeman said, "I never thought you would invite me to eat with you."

"So you remember what happened when I was a little boy?" asked Dele.

"Yes, I remember," answered the policeman.

"I promised then that I would kill you," said Dele, "because you killed my little sister. But Jesus has shown me that I must forgive you instead. I am praying that God will forgive you, too."

The policeman's eyes filled with tears. "I want to ask God to

forgive me, too," he said. "I didn't want to do it, but I followed the chief's orders anyway. Because of that I killed your sister."

Together the men bowed their heads, and Don Manuel prayed that Nsiamindele and the policeman would be able to let go of their old hatreds. When the two men lifted their heads, they smiled at each other. Their hearts were filled with happiness.

And now, instead of an enemy, Dele had a new friend.

Nsiamindele was born in Kikaka, Angola, in the early 1900s. He was baptized as a Christian on December 4, 1932. This story from his life was adapted from the book They Loved Their Enemies *by Marian Hostetler (Herald Press, 1988).*

Josh, the Repairman

It was a sunny afternoon in Alabama. In a small-town grocery store on Maple Street, Danny Armstrong was watching his father.

"What's the matter, Daddy?" he asked. Mr. Armstrong's kind, brown face was ridged with worry as he bent over the low, open refrigerator.

"Oh, this thing's not working right again, son," he answered,

"It's got to be fixed—can't afford to let the food spoil."

Danny knew Daddy was right. When you run a grocery store, you have to sell fresh food. That's the first rule. Danny knew lots of things about the grocery business. Every day after school he worked in the store. So did his brothers and sisters. Mama, who was there all day, said she couldn't get along without them.

Now Danny wondered what the problem was. It seemed like a man had just been there to fix the refrigerator.

"What're you gonna do?" he asked his daddy, "Gonna get someone to come fix it again?"

Daddy looked at Danny but didn't answer right away. Finally he said sadly, "That's just the trouble, son. I don't think anyone will come."

"Why not?" asked Danny.

Daddy hesitated, then he said slowly, "You know, Danny, how I'm trying to get elected to the city council?"

Danny nodded.

"That's the group that makes the laws for our city. They make the rules for the police, the fire department, the schools—things like that."

Danny nodded, again, wondering what Daddy was leading up to.

"Well, son, some white people don't like it that I'm trying to get on the council. They think a black man like me should stick to running his grocery store. They don't want black folks making rules for them."

"Why not, Daddy?" asked Danny.

"I think they're kind of scared. Because some white people have treated black people badly, I think they're afraid we'll try to make things bad for them if we have the chance. They think I'll try to cause trouble if I get on the council."

Danny looked into his father's kind, dark eyes. He knew his daddy wouldn't do anything like that.

Daddy went on, "When Mr. Johnson was here to fix this

refrigerator the other day, he let me know he wasn't very happy to be here. He hinted that I wouldn't be able to get my machines fixed anymore as long as I was running for city council. I guess he's right, too. I already called three other repairmen, and they all had excuses for not coming."

"What're you gonna do, Daddy?" asked Danny. "Let the food spoil?"

"No, Danny. Can't do that," said Daddy, tiredly. Then he smiled and rubbed Danny's head. "I think I'll call one more repairman I never hired before. I heard he's a religious man. Maybe he'll help."

Danny watched hopefully as Daddy dialed the phone. He wished hard that the man would come. What if he too said no? Would Daddy give up the idea of being on city council? He hoped not. He knew how much Daddy wanted to make their city a better place—for everyone.

Across town, the phone rang at Josh Watson's home. He answered cheerfully, as always. Josh wasn't surprised to hear Danny's father on the line. The other refrigerator repairmen in town had warned him to expect a call from Mr. Armstrong. They had also warned Josh not to help him.

"If he sees he can't keep his grocery store running, maybe he'll drop his crazy idea of getting on city council," they said. "We don't need a black man telling us what to do."

Josh had told them he didn't see any reason not to repair a man's machines just because he had dark skin. The other men didn't say much, but he could tell they were angry.

Now Mr. Armstrong was asking him for help. Josh was a follower of Jesus, and he knew what Jesus would do. Still he was afraid. Would the other repairmen try to hurt him or his family if he didn't listen to them? Bad things had happened before to folks who took a black person's side.

Quickly Josh breathed a prayer to God. "Help me to have courage," he prayed. Then he said aloud, "Sure, Mr. Armstrong, I can come now. I'll be right over."

When Josh examined the refrigerator in the Armstrongs' grocery store, he found loosened gas lines at the back. The first repairman had fixed the machine, all right. He had fixed it to break down!

Danny saw the angry looks on his daddy's face and on Josh's face as they talked about it.

"I'm so sorry that people think they have to act like this," said Josh. "They just can't seem to get along with anyone who's a little bit different from them."

"That's okay," answered Danny's father, a smile spreading over his face. "We know not everyone feels like they do. I sure am glad to have found a new repairman today!" He held out his hand, and Josh shook it warmly.

"I'm glad to be your repairman," he replied, "whenever you need me.

"And your friend, too," he added, with a wink at Danny.

Josh Watson (not his real name) never did have trouble with the other repairmen after he fixed Mr. Armstrong's refrigerator. In fact, the grocery store's regular repairman tried to get his job back again. Mr. Armstrong was elected to city council that year and remained a member for many years.

Bonnie, Follower of Jesus

Chug, chug, chug. The engine of the old truck sputtered as Bonnie Cumming drove over the rough road of Poundmaker Reservation in Saskatchewan.

What's wrong with this thing now? she wondered. Chug . . . chug. The truck gave one last cough and stopped dead.

Oh, no! thought Bonnie, *It can't be out of gas! I just filled the tank yesterday. Didn't I?* Out of habit she checked the gas gauge, but it was no help. It was broken.

With a sigh, Bonnie jumped out of the truck and looked into the gas tank. *It looks empty*, she thought. *How can that be?* She checked the ground to see if gas had leaked out, but she couldn't see anything.

Later that day, Bonnie told a friend, "I'm sure I filled the gas tank yesterday. What could have happened?"

"Maybe someone drained it out of your tank and stole it," suggested her friend.

Stole it! What an awful thought. It made Bonnie feel afraid. Did someone need gas that badly? Or did they just want to be mean to her?

Bonnie was new on the reservation. She had come as a volunteer with Mennonite Central Committee to help the Native people plant gardens. She also worked with the teenagers, taking them to socials and meetings. Could it be that they didn't want her there? Did they want her to go back where she came from?

Bonnie worried, but she kept on with her gardening projects and working with the youth. She was careful to keep her truck full of gas.

Then a few days later it happened again. Chug, chug, splutter. Out of gas. This time Bonnie was a little bit angry, but she did nothing about it—except to put more gas in the truck.

A week after that, the gas was stolen again. Now Bonnie was really getting mad.

The night before she took a group of teenagers on a canoe trip, she had to sleep in the truck to make sure there would be gas for the trip in the morning. Her bones ached, and she felt tired. *This thief sure is making life hard for me*, she thought.

Gas kept disappearing from the tank. Bonnie bought a gas cap that could be locked, but the thief only ruined it trying to pry it open. She had to ask someone to help her get the broken cap off.

Two months had passed. Bonnie was sick and tired of the whole thing. Gas had been stolen from her truck ten times. She and a friend began to think of ways to get even with the thief.

"I know!" said her friend, "I'll mix sugar with the gas. When the thief puts *that* in his engine, it'll wreck it!"

Bonnie and her friend laughed gleefully together. It would serve that thief right! Bonnie decided to do it. She went to the community leaders to ask them if it would be okay. They said yes. She checked with the police, and they thought it was a good idea.

Everything was all set. The plan was ready to go, except that somehow Bonnie didn't feel right about it. *The thief deserves it,* she tried to tell herself. *It'll teach him a lesson.* Still she couldn't bring herself to do it.

What would Jesus do? she wondered. *I don't think he would set a trap and try to get back at the thief.*

"God, what shall I do?" Bonnie prayed. Soon she thought of a new idea.

That night she taped a note to the gas cap on the truck, along with a $10 bill. The note said, "If you need the gas that bad, take the money. If you don't have enough money, come see me. I'll see if I can help you find a job. I need this gas to do my gardening work and take youth on trips."

Bonnie went to bed feeling good and slept better than she had in a long time.

In the morning the gas and the money were still there, and no one ever stole gas from Bonnie again.

Bonnie Cumming, Dunster, British Columbia, knew God had helped her to do the right thing. If she had ruined the thief's engine with sugar gas, it would have "started an all-out war." This story was adapted from the article "What Would Christ Do?" by John Longhurst, Gospel Herald *(May 30, 1989).*

Harry, the Butcher

It was Saturday morning in Mount Joy, Pennsylvania. Sunlight streamed through the large glass windows of Harry Krall's butcher shop, lighting up the white meat cases and making the countertop shine.

Dick, Harry's teenage grandson, hurried to wrap a package of steaks for a customer. There were two

45

more people waiting in his line. *Just like every Saturday,* he thought to himself, *always busy.*

Dick gave change to the customer and took a moment to push up his glasses. They were always sliding down his hot, sweaty nose. He glanced over at Grandpa and his uncle and aunt, who were working behind the counter too. They were as busy as he was.

It was hard work at Grandpa's butcher shop, but Dick enjoyed it. He loved the gleaming counters and refrigerator cases. He loved the cold, meaty smell of the store. He even loved waiting on customers and getting to know them. But most of all he loved Grandpa.

Grandpa Krall made the butcher shop special. Grandpa had white hair and a kind face with twinkly eyes. He loved to tell jokes and stories, and Dick loved to listen. It was Grandpa who taught Dick how to treat customers—honestly and with respect. But he never scolded. Grandpa just explained things in a kind, friendly way that made Dick feel like pleasing him.

Dick smiled a little now as he watched Grandpa talking with a customer. He was telling another story, his eyes twinkling merrily. Dick turned back to his own work. The time went fast when there were lots of customers, and he soon noticed that the sun was creeping higher in the sky.

Suddenly Dick heard a familiar booming voice. Looking up, he saw jolly Mr. Porter coming in the door. Mr. Porter was one of Grandpa's good friends and a regular customer at the butcher shop. He was a businessman, with plenty of money. He always wore a suit which strained around his short, stout body.

Dick guessed that Mr. Porter was there to buy a roast for Sunday dinner, or maybe for company that evening. Mr. Porter always bought the best meat, the most tender and delicious. He could afford it, and Grandpa was happy to give advice on what was the best.

But today, before Mr. Porter could get to the counter, Grandpa hurried over to him. "I need to talk to you," he said. "I owe you an apology."

Mr. Porter looked surprised and puzzled. "An apology? What for?"

Dick knew this was none of his business and he shouldn't pay attention to what the two men were saying, but his ears just kept listening.

"Remember last week when you bought that nice, big roast?" Grandpa asked. Mr. Porter nodded, and Grandpa went on. "When you went out the door you called back and said, 'Now that isn't bull beef, is it?' "

Mr. Porter said, "Yes, I remember. And you assured me it wasn't."

"Well, I don't know what made me say that," said Grandpa, his eyes moist with tears, "because it was. It *was* meat from a bull, and I lied to you. It's been worrying me all week."

For a few seconds Mr. Porter didn't say a word. Dick watched anxiously. What was he going to do?

Then Mr. Porter's great laugh rang out. He put his hand on Grandpa's shoulder. "Is *that* all you've been worried about,

Harry?" he said. "Whatever that meat was, it sure was good—excellent!"

Dick let out his breath, and at the same moment he saw Grandpa relax and sigh, as if a heavy weight had been lifted from his shoulders. Then Mr. Porter and Grandpa headed for the counter, and he quickly looked back at his work.

All his young life, Dick had learned at home and at church that Jesus wants his followers to be truthful. In his mind he understood that. But that day in the butcher shop he saw an example he would never forget. He saw how telling the truth made his grandpa feel, and how it made Mr. Porter feel. He knew in his heart that he would try to always be honest—like Jesus, and like Grandpa.

Dick Krall learned from both his grandpa and his father to be honest and treat others fairly and kindly. When he grew up and became a book salesman, he tried to follow their example with all his customers.

Unselfish Kathryn

"Now, Kathryn, stand still!" said Mama, as she finished tying a ribbon onto her braids.

Kathryn stood as still as she could and smiled at her sister, Bertha. Today she hadn't even cried when Mama combed through her tangled curls. It was Sunday, and Kathryn and Bertha were wearing their new dresses to church.

The sisters weren't twins, but they were so close in age that Mama often dressed them alike. She made their dresses herself, and always added a little something extra to make them special.

On this winter morning Kathryn and Bertha couldn't help smiling, because their new dresses were even prettier than usual. They were made from soft wool, in a clear blue color, and they had white lace collars. To set them off, Mama had tied big white satin bows in their hair. They could hardly wait for the other girls at church to see them.

Soon they were rumbling along in the buggy to Forks Church. Ahead of them, Kathryn's older brothers rode in a separate buggy. Their family was too large to fit in just one.

Bertha jostled against Kathryn as they drove over a bump and gave her a kind smile. Then she turned away to look out over the frozen fields. *Bertha's always so good,* Kathryn thought to herself, *She always does the right thing. I wish I could be like that.*

Then she decided that maybe today she could be as good as Bertha, because she felt so happy in her new dress. As the buggy wheels spun on down the road to church, drumming a rhythm in her ears, Kathryn decided she would be as good as gold today. All day long she would be unselfish, kind, and obedient. It shouldn't be too hard on Sunday.

Gravel scrunched under the buggy wheels. They were pulling into the churchyard. Of course, they were almost the first ones there, because Father was the preacher. Kathryn and Bertha could hardly wait for their friends to arrive.

The wait was worth it. "Oh, what beautiful dresses!" the other girls squealed. "Did your mother really make them? They look store-bought!"

Kathryn was in her glory. She turned around and swirled her skirts, showing off—until she noticed Bertha standing there smiling. Then she remembered her promise to herself to be good. It wasn't nice to be so proud. So Kathryn, too, smiled quietly at the other girls.

An hour later she felt herself getting sleepy as she listened to Father's sermon. The bench felt awfully hard, but she reminded herself that good girls listened in church.

Suddenly there was a commotion at the back of the room. Several men began jumping up and putting on their coats. Someone announced that a neighbor's house was on fire, and the men were going to help put it out.

From then on, it was not a usual Sunday. It was hard to concentrate on Father's preaching. Kathryn sat up straight to look out the window. But she couldn't see any fire. How scary it would be to watch your house burn!

Later when Kathryn and her family sat down to enjoy Mama's good Sunday dinner, they could talk of nothing but the fire. Mama was concerned about the owners of the house, who had lost almost everything. They had gone to stay with family, but they would still need things like clothing.

"You know," said Mama, "I believe that family has two girls, about the age of you two girls." She looked at Kathryn and Bertha.

Kathryn stopped chewing her bite of roast chicken.

Something about the way Mama was looking at her made her feel worried.

"I think it would be nice if you girls would each give them one dress," Mama went on. Her face grew thoughtful. "You know, it's awfully cold. Those new wool dresses of yours would keep them warm this winter."

Kathryn and Bertha stared at Mama. Kathryn swallowed her food with a gulp and almost choked on it. Her beautiful blue dress was now hanging in her room upstairs, but Kathryn could picture every detail of it in her mind. Soft blue wool. Crisp white lace. How could she give up that dress?

Now Bertha was speaking. "All right, Mama, I'll give my new dress," she said quietly.

Mama smiled. "I know Jesus will be pleased. You know, he wants us to give our best." Her eyes moved to Kathryn.

Kathryn squirmed. She felt miserable. It wasn't fair! If she gave up her new dress, she would only have one Sunday dress all winter.

Then she remembered the promise she had made to herself in the buggy. All day long she would be unselfish, kind, and obedient. Maybe this was Jesus' way of helping her keep her promise. And she did feel sorry for those girls.

Swallowing hard, she blurted out, "Me, too—I mean, I will give my new dress, too!"

Mama smiled warmly at her, and suddenly Kathryn didn't care about having only one Sunday dress. She felt relieved and happy.

She had pleased Mama and Jesus, and she had kept her own promise. She could just imagine the look on that other girl's face when she saw the beautiful blue wool dress!

This story of Kathryn Miller and her sister, Bertha, took place near Middlebury, Indiana, around the year 1910. Kathryn's father, D. D. Miller, was an evangelist and pastor of the South Forks Church. In 1918, Kathryn moved to Iowa to teach school. She later married and raised a family there.

Mildred, Loving Mother

It was a beautiful, sunny day. Mildred looked out her kitchen window as she washed the breakfast dishes. *How blue the sky is today,* she thought. She watched the fluffy, white clouds drift by.

Outside in the sandbox, little Rodney was happily driving his trucks and tractor through the

54

sand. The hood of his jacket had fallen back, and his light brown hair shone in the sunlight.

As Mildred finished the dishes, she noticed Peter, the small neighbor boy, running over. Soon he was playing with Rodney in his sandbox.

The boys were having a good time, and Mildred left the window to make a batch of cookies. She had just taken the first trays out of the oven when she heard Rodney screaming.

"Mommy! Mommy!" she heard him cry. Mildred hurried out the back door, a pot holder still in her hand.

Rodney hurled himself into her arms, sobbing. Peter had disappeared.

For a few minutes Rodney just clung to his mother. His little body shook with sobs. Finally he wiggled free from her arms and looked at her.

"Mommy!" he said, tears still running from his wide, brown eyes, "Mommy, Pete said he's going to shoot me. He's got a gun!"

A gun? thought Mildred. *No wonder Rodney is so scared. He's not used to guns, even toy guns.* She patted his back. "You'll be all right, Rodney," she said soothingly. "Peter can't really shoot you. It's only a toy."

Mildred looked around for the neighbor boy. She couldn't see him anywhere. "Pete!" she called. "Please come here, Pete!" She tried to sound pleasant so he would know she wasn't angry with him. "Pete! I want to talk to you!"

It was no use. The boy was hiding and was afraid to come out.

Suddenly Mildred had an idea. "Come, Rodney," she said, taking his hand. "Let's go get some cookies for you and Pete."

Rodney came willingly. He was ready to play with his friend again. Mildred watched from the kitchen window as he left the house with two cookies.

As if by magic, Pete appeared again. Soon the two small boys were sitting on the steps in the sunshine, munching their treat.

Mildred went about her work in the kitchen. She was glad that things were peaceful again in the backyard. Before long, though, she heard Rodney screaming and crying.

Glancing out the window, she saw that Pete had his toy gun out. He was pointing it at Rodney.

Quickly she dashed out the door, hoping to catch Pete this time. But she was too late. Pete was gone.

As she comforted Rodney, Mildred thought hard. *Somehow, I have to let Pete know that Rodney is really afraid of his gun. I have to tell him that we don't allow guns at our house, even if they are only toys.* "Dear God," she prayed, "please give me a chance to talk to Pete. Please help him to know that I'm not angry with him."

Once again, Mildred thought of cookies. "How about some more cookies, Rod?" she asked cheerfully. Soon little Rodney was back in the yard with two more cookies.

Pete appeared again, and the boys were happy for a short time. Then Pete had gotten his toy gun again, and Rodney was crying.

When Mildred rushed outside, Pete was gone, as usual. This time she didn't feel much like being pleasant. But she knew Jesus wouldn't give up.

I'll try once more to talk to Pete, she thought. *God will help me.*

Rodney was willing to share another cookie with Pete. In a few minutes the boys were getting along again. Mildred decided to go talk to Pete while the boys were still eating. This time he didn't run away.

Mildred explained why Rodney was so afraid. She asked him to take his gun home and leave it there.

Pete did take his gun home. After that, the two boys became good friends. They played together often and were so close they even had chicken pox together.

And Pete never brought a gun to Rodney's house again.

Mildred Zook, Minot, North Dakota, watched Rodney and his friend, Peter, grow up together. They remained fast friends through their high school years. Later Rodney became a Mennonite pastor.

Aaron, the Peacemaker

The Lehmans' 1937 black Chevy chugged down the gravel farm lane. Louie looked out the window at the rows of emerald green corn rippling in the breeze. Sunlight shone through the tassels, making them glow. It was a perfect summer evening. Louie squirmed uncomfortably in his stiff starched Sunday shirt and wool knee pants. He knew it would be hot in the Sonnenberg Church, but Aaron, Louie's dad, was the song leader. Their family always went to the evening service. And they went early.

They were a little late this time, and Dad kept his foot on the gas. Being on time was almost as important as being godly and clean.

Louie took his mind off the heat by watching birds and rabbits out the car window. Finally they reached the end of the lane. Dad was just about to turn onto the road when he hesitated. Coming toward them, very slowly, was an old pickup truck.

That's Joe Bates! thought Louie. *He's probably up to no good.* The whole neighborhood knew that Joe stole gas from people's farm tanks when they were gone. He threatened to shoot people who came onto his property. And he didn't think much of Christians, especially "Sunday-go-to-meetin' Mennonites."

Dad didn't wait for Joe's pickup to drive past the lane. Instead he pulled out onto the road and headed for church, as usual. But when they reached the Kidron Pike, instead of turning right to go to church, Dad turned left.

What's going on? wondered Louie in surprise. He and Martha and Freeman sat on the edge of the back seat and looked at each other excitedly.

Mother raised her eyebrows at Dad and asked, "Aaron, where are you planning to go now?"

"Leave it to me," he replied. "I'll take care of everything."

This was not like Dad at all. They were going to be late for church! Dad drove through the countryside, around a big square, up and down the hills and hollows and back to their farm.

When they turned the last corner, they saw Joe's old pickup parked near the large, white corncrib. "I believe Joe is taking our corn for his pigs," said Dad, matter-of-factly.

With large eyes, Louie, Martha, and Freeman stared out the window toward the corncrib. Joe had backed his truck right up to the door. Quietly, Dad drove up in front of Joe's pickup, turned off the motor, and got out of the car.

By this time, they could tell Mother was worried. She squeezed her hands tightly together in her lap. She and the children watched anxiously as Dad walked calmly over to the corncrib. What if Joe had his gun with him?

Thud! They heard a big shovelful of corn hit the bed of Joe's truck. Dad was right! He was stealing corn.

As Joe's face appeared in the open doorway of the corncrib, Dad called out cheerfully, "Keep on shoveling, Joe! If you need more tomorrow, come on back and get some. You're welcome to as much as you need. Don't forget, you're my neighbor!"

With a blank look of surprise, Joe stopped shoveling. When he realized what Dad was saying, he hung his head. He dropped his shovel and said nothing.

Dad hopped back in the car. Without looking back, the family drove to church.

That was the last time Joe ever took corn from the Lehmans. The neighbors had no more trouble with stolen gas, either. And from that time on, Louie was never afraid of Joe.

Louie Lehman, Albany, Oregon, grew up to be a minister. In later years he remembered nothing about the sermon preached that night at Sonnenberg Church in Kidron, Ohio, but he never forgot what his father, Aaron, did. He called it a "living sermon."

Peter, Brave Teacher

It was a cold December morning in Russia in 1924. In the schoolroom of a small village, teacher Peter Konrad stood before his pupils. He nodded his head slowly as he talked, his eyes peering through heavy, gold-rimmed glasses.

"Children," he said sadly, "today I must tell you that the government has made a new rule. We are not allowed to have any Christmas programs in the schools."

Peter stopped talking for a moment. He could see the surprise and disappointment

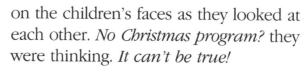

on the children's faces as they looked at each other. *No Christmas program?* they were thinking. *It can't be true!*

The townspeople always gathered at the school to celebrate Christmas Eve. They sang carols and listened joyfully as Peter told the story of Jesus' birth. Now they were forbidden to have this special time.

Peter continued, "It's hard for us to understand why things like this happen, but God still loves us and will always be with us. Because of God's love Jesus was born. We can celebrate his birthday in our hearts."

The children were unusually quiet as they trudged home from school. Soon news of the rule had spread to everyone in town.

On the morning before Christmas, Peter's best friend, Jakob Schmidt, came right after breakfast to see him. He had tried hard to think of a way for the children to have their Christmas celebration. He thought it might work to have a program in his barn.

"Anna and I have agreed," Jakob said. "If we build a fire in the little iron stove and keep it going all afternoon, the barn will be warm enough."

Peter was excited to think of having a celebration after all, but he knew it would be dangerous. If the government found out about the program, there might be trouble.

"Are you sure you want to do this, Jakob?" he asked.

"Yes, Peter," answered Jakob. "We'll keep it a secret. But you are the one who will be in charge. Do you think it's the right thing?"

"It is right for the children to celebrate Christmas," Peter said slowly, "and God will be with us, no matter what happens."

The message about the secret program flew through the village. When the children got to school, they were bursting with happiness. Eagerly they practiced songs and speeches for the special event.

It grew dark early that Christmas Eve. One by one the oil lamps in the houses went out, as people walked along the wet streets to Jakob Schmidt's barn. Soon the whole village was dark.

In the barn two hundred men, women, and children sat quietly in piles of hay, waiting for Peter to begin. The only light came from two lanterns hung above the homemade stage. In the rafters pigeons cooed, and from the cow stables came contented munching sounds.

In a calm voice, teacher Peter began to read from the Bible. "And she wrapped him in swaddling clothes, and laid him in a manger, because there was no room for them in the inn."

He paused. Everyone was silent, listening to the stable sounds and thinking about the first Christmas. . . .

Meanwhile, back in the village, a man came riding through the dark streets. Not one of the houses had a light. He stopped in front of the school and listened carefully. From somewhere he heard the sound of children singing, floating softly on the night air. He waited a few minutes, then turned his horse and rode away.

In the barn, the last song had been sung, and the last verse recited. Tall and thin, teacher Peter Konrad stood up to say goodnight.

"Dear friends," he said. "These are hard times. God is the only one who knows if we will see each other again. But whatever happens, we know that

Jesus promised to always be with us. Take that promise home with you, and God bless you all."

It was late when Peter left the stable. He was alone, but he felt happy and peaceful as he walked to his rooms. He was not afraid of what might happen.

At midnight, Peter woke up with a start. Someone was knocking at his door. When he opened it, he saw men on horseback.

A rough voice told him to dress quickly and pack whatever he could carry. Peter did as he was told. Then the men made him walk ahead of them down the muddy street.

None of his friends ever saw Peter Konrad again. No one was sure what happened to him, but they always remembered what he said in the barn that Christmas Eve. And they remembered that wherever Peter was, Jesus was always with him.

This story about the brave teacher, Peter Konrad, was first written by John Goerz, one of his pupils. Later it was retold by Betty Miller and has been adapted by permission.

Lois, Wartime Helper

The big ship rocked gently back and forth on the waves. Lois stood on the deck and gazed out at the moonlit sea. As far as she could see there was water—miles and miles of water, shimmering under the big night sky.

How peaceful it seemed! It was hard for Lois to remember that at the end of her journey was a war, a big war that was changing her life.

With every chug of its big engines, the ship pulled her farther across the Atlantic

Ocean, from her home in Indiana to southern France, to the very edge of the fighting.

Only a month ago Lois had heard about the refugees there. They were Jews who had left their home countries because they were no longer safe. The soldiers who now walked the streets of their hometowns did not like Jewish people. The Jews knew that if they stayed they would be sent to concentration camps like many of their friends. They knew people died in those camps.

Many Jewish families escaped secretly to southern France. Because they came as fast as they could, with no time and no room to bring many belongings, they were poor and had few clothes.

Some of these families found their way to Rivesaltes (Reev-zault′), a refugee camp. There they lived together in long buildings with rows of beds. They ate their meals, mostly bread and soup, sitting on benches at long tables.

When Lois heard about the refugees, she wanted to help. When she heard there was a home for refugee children that needed a director, someone who spoke French, she knew this was how she could help. Lois was young and strong—and a French teacher.

Lois knew it was dangerous to go to France now, but she believed God was telling her to help the children there. She felt ready to face whatever might happen.

So Lois packed her bags; said good-by to her father, mother, sisters, and brothers; and sailed from New York City.

Finally the voyage was over. Lois arrived at the large,

three-story home, Villa St. Cristophe (Veel-a Sa Krees-toff'). She was greeted by a houseful of children, from four to fifteen years old. They called her "Mademoiselle." In front of the house was a wide, sandy beach, bordered by the beautiful blue water of the Mediterranean Sea.

Gradually Lois learned to know the children and settled into the daily routine. The days were filled with lessons in the classroom, good meals, walks, and games along the beach. After supper came story hour, then bedtime. Lois was so glad she could help the home run smoothly and make life a little happier for these children!

When Lois handed out letters to the children from their families at Camp Rivesaltes, it was a favorite time of the day. But when children no longer received mail, they knew the soldiers had found their parents and taken them away and they might never hear from them again. The soldiers were always looking for persons who had escaped to France without special permission papers.

One day when the children were out on their morning walk, Lois heard a loud rapping at the door. Opening it, she found herself facing two policemen. They said they had come for eight-year-old Louise, her six-year-old brother, Armand, and their little sister, Monique.

Oh, no! thought Lois, *I can't let them take the children!* She knew this was bad news for them—that soldiers would be waiting to take them away.

Lois prayed quietly then said, as calmly as she could, "The children are on their morning walk. They will not be back until lunchtime."

The policemen left but said they would be back after lunch. Lois thanked God for this extra time. "Please help me find a way to keep the officers from taking the children," she prayed.

At two o'clock the policemen returned. They asked Lois to pack the children's clothes and turn the three over to them.

Thinking quickly she replied, "I cannot possibly pack their clothes now, because the laundry woman is doing the washing. Their clothes are wet and will not be dry until late afternoon!"

As Lois watched for the men's reaction, she silently asked God to help her keep the children longer. To her surprise, the policemen agreed to leave and return later, about suppertime.

Lois had bargained for a little more time, but there wasn't much more she could do to keep the soldiers away from the children. *It's in God's hands now*, she thought.

At five o'clock the officers came to the door again. They said they had received word from another office to wait for some papers they needed to show her. They would return later in the evening. Lois was to have the children all packed and ready to go.

Tick, tick, tick. The hands moved slowly around the clock. At last it was bedtime. The policemen had not come. Louise, Armand, and Monique finally went to sleep in their usual places. Even the grown-ups gave up their watch and went to bed.

The next morning, as early sunlight shone on the blue water and sparkling sand, a message arrived at the home from the police. Special papers had come from a Frenchman, a friend of the children. Because the papers gave the children permission to live in France, the soldiers could never take them away!

Everyone was so happy that Louise and Armand and Monique were there to stay! And Lois knew that God had heard their prayers.

Lois Gunden Clemens directed the Mennonite refugee children's home, Villa St. Christophe, from 1941 to the end of 1942. In January 1943, soldiers captured her. Along with other Americans, Lois was taken into Germany and held prisoner for thirteen months in a large hotel. She returned to the United States in 1944, where she resumed her teaching.

Beth, Kind Friend

Beth stared out the window of the yellow school bus as it rumbled along the road toward home. Usually she felt peaceful and happy watching the stream, the cornfields, and the woods go by. But today she didn't really see anything. Beth's eyes were filled with tears, and the sound of shouting drummed in her ears.

One of the neighborhood girls, Greta, was yelling at her. She didn't even know why. Greta was calling her a "goody-goody." "You think

you're better than everyone else!" she accused.

Beth was afraid to turn around and look at Greta.

Ouch! She felt a jab on her shoulder from behind. It was Greta. "What's the matter? Scared to turn around?" she sneered.

"Leave her alone!" Beth's big sister, Lois, said loudly from across the aisle. Greta just laughed, and her sister Lori joined in. It was an ugly sound.

Now Beth was really scared. Several times girls had started fights on the bus and hit each other hard. What if Greta hit her now?

Desperately Beth tried to plan what to do. Soon she would be home, but Greta and Lori got off at the same stop. She couldn't escape right away.

Beth knew what her father would say. Dad would tell her to just walk away. "Don't say anything unkind, and don't hit back." It was the rule she and Lois had grown up with. It was the rule Mom and Dad lived by.

In all her nine years, Beth had never seen her mother and father be unkind to anyone. They welcomed strangers into their home, and Dad was always ready to give rides to people who needed them. Several times people had stolen things from their house and car, but Dad was never discouraged.

Beth remembered that once when their car was extra full, Dad passed by a hitchhiker. As they drove on he told the family how bad he felt that he hadn't stopped to pick up the man.

"Why?" asked the children, wondering where they could have made room.

"Because that was Jesus walking along the road," he replied.

That's how Dad feels, thought Beth now. *He says we should treat everyone as if they were Jesus.* But Greta? How could she think of Greta as Jesus? It would be so much easier just to hit her back.

Beth knew Greta and her sister, Lori, well. She and Lois often played with them. The two girls were hard to get along with, and they sometimes cheated at games.

When Beth and Lois complained, Dad felt bad for them, but he always said, "Try to be kind to Lori and Greta. They have a harder life than we do, you know."

Beth knew it was true. She had heard Greta's parents fighting. Her father drank alcohol and had a bad temper. Because he didn't have a steady job, the family was poor. If Beth thought about it that way, she could think of Greta as someone to help instead of as an enemy.

Just then the bus stopped, jerking her from her thoughts. It was time to get off.

She could hear Greta still muttering mean things about her. Lois turned to give Beth a sympathetic look as they headed for the front of the bus.

Now Beth knew what she would do, but she still felt afraid. "Please help me, God," she prayed silently. As she walked down the aisle she could feel Greta pushing close behind her.

As soon as the bus doors closed behind them, Greta began shouting at Beth again. Then she gave Beth's hair a hard yank.

It hurt badly, but Beth didn't turn around. Blinking fast to keep from crying, she kept walking toward home. She could almost feel the girl's eyes burning through her back. Would Greta follow?

Beth wanted to run, but something told her just to walk. The sidewalk to their house seemed endless. Finally Beth reached the door. There was her mother, smiling, ready to hear about her day.

Suddenly Beth felt light and happy. She smiled back. God had helped her do the right thing.

Beth and her sister, Lois, continued to play with Greta and Lori until they moved away. The girls even joined Beth's family for worship sometimes.

Beth Newcomer, Scottdale, Pennsylvania, grew up to be the mother of three children. She was happy to share with them this story of when she followed her parents' example.

Beth's father, Ivan Moon, an artist, and her mother, Naomi, worked as volunteers for many years in their church's food pantry, helping people in need.

Brave Rose Marie

Tap, tap, tap! The knock on the door sounded urgent. Rose Marie Biddier, not waiting for a servant to come, opened the door herself.

A young messenger stood in the darkness, breathing hard.

"There is shooting at the prime minister's house!" he gasped. "I have run three miles to warn you. Mr. Biddier must leave—now!"

Quickly Rose Marie let the young man in and gave him a chair to sit on. Her thoughts raced as she listened to his story.

Kwami, her husband, belonged to the prime minister's cabinet, which made him an important official in the government of Ghana. He had told her there might be trouble. Last week Kwami had voted against the man who became commander of the army because he did not trust him.

Now the prime minister was far away in Great Britain, and the new commander was using his soldiers to take over the government and rule the country himself. Because Kwami had voted against him, the commander was angry and would come to punish him.

Hurriedly Rose Marie gathered important papers and packed a few clothes for her husband. Kwami was on the the telephone, warning friends.

Suddenly he tapped the phone again and again. "It's dead," he exclaimed. "The lines have been cut. We must go!"

Leaving their children with servants and relatives in the house, Rose Marie and Kwami hurried to an American official's house. The first streaks of daylight were spreading across the sky. As she drove, Rose Marie thanked God that their car was not a big fancy government vehicle. Maybe no one would recognize them.

Just then a truckload of soldiers came toward them on the road. Rose Marie held her breath. But the soldiers passed by. "Thank you, God," she prayed.

When Kwami was safe with the Americans, Rose Marie returned home. Trying to keep calm, she packed things for herself and the children.

She heard a noise outside. Looking out the window, she saw a truckload of soldiers racing to the house.

Quickly she rounded up the servants and her husband's relatives. "Go!" she cried. "Escape while you can!"

But they stared at her, frightened and helpless. No one would leave.

In minutes the soldiers had taken over the house. Rose Marie, her family, and all the servants were called to the courtyard. There the soldiers surrounded them, pointing loaded rifles at them.

"Who are you? Why are you here?" a rough voice demanded. A soldier was talking to Kwami's uncle.

The old man was too frightened to speak.

"Answer me!" shouted the young soldier, thrusting his bayonet at the old man.

The uncle collapsed into a chair, shaking.

"Please," cried Rose Marie, "please, he is one of my husband's uncles and is staying here. He has nothing to do with the government! Here, let *me* tell you who all these people are."

The leader nodded.

In a clear voice, Rose Marie gave the names of the servants, of Kwami's relatives, and of her children—Peter, Sofia, and Joel. For one strange minute, she felt almost as if the soldiers were her guests, standing there in the courtyard among the green vines and brilliant blossoms.

But then the leader of the soldiers ordered the children to move back. He began to question Rose Marie.

She felt a stab of fear. What would happen now? She saw the young soldiers, pacing the courtyard with their guns ready. They were tense and anxious. Any little thing might set them off.

Rose Marie looked at her children and the other members of her household. They were so frightened! She knew she must be brave for them. God would help her.

"Please," she said gently to the head soldier. "We are not going anywhere, and we are not armed. I will answer your questions."

Quickly the man ordered his soldiers to lower their guns. "Is it true," he asked, "that you drove your husband away?"

"Yes," answered Rose Marie.

"Where have you taken him?"

"To the Americans. He has done nothing wrong, and he doesn't deserve to be treated this way."

"If he has done nothing wrong," asked the soldier, "why is he running?"

"If he has done nothing wrong, why are you chasing him?" retorted Rose Marie.

Some of the young soldiers laughed and the leader tensed.

I must be careful, thought Rose Marie. *He does not like to be embarrassed in front of his men. If he gets angry, he may hurt someone.*

"Where is your husband?" asked the soldier.

"I do not know."

"But you drove him!"

"Yes," answered Rose Marie, "but we knew it would not be wise for me to know. When I dropped him off at the Americans' house, they moved him to safety. If I knew where he was, then you could force me to tell, so isn't it better for me not to know?"

Finally the soldier said, "We have to make sure he is not here."

"Go ahead," said Rose Marie. To the head servant she said, "Attia, show them all the rooms."

When the soldiers had finished searching, their leader said to Rose Marie, "We have to arrest you for taking him away."

So they are going to punish me after all! she thought, her head spinning. *I must think what to do!*

Quickly she turned to Attia, saying, "Go get the passports. You and Sofie take the children to the Americans."

As the servant left, Rose Marie, forcing her voice to be calm, asked, "All right, where are we going?"

"Why should you know?" the soldier demanded.

"To tell the Americans where I am."

"I must leave some soldiers here," the man said. "We will

76

come for you in the morning."

When the head soldier had left, Rose Marie took a deep breath and looked around at the soldiers left behind. She did not know what would happen to her tomorrow, but she knew what she would do today. Jesus said, "Be kind to everyone, even your enemies." She had learned that as a little girl, far away in Kidron, Ohio.

Calling the servants, she asked them to take coffee and cake to the soldiers. Later she served them breakfast. The men looked at her with surprise and wonder. After that they treated her more gently.

Time went on. No one came to arrest Rose Marie. When the soldiers guarding the house were replaced with new men, she gave them food.

Several times people came and searched the house to see if Kwami had returned. But the soldiers protected Rose Marie and her household and guarded her property.

One day she and her children were able to leave Ghana. They flew to the United States, where Kwami joined them six months later. Together Rose Marie and her family thanked God for being with them and helping them show love even when their lives were in danger.

Rose Marie Amstutz was a social worker in Chicago when she met and married Kwami Biddier. They returned to his native country, Ghana, where he was Secretary of Agriculture. When the government was overthrown and they fled to the United States, the family settled in College Park, Maryland. Rose Marie became a science teacher, and Kwami, who later became blind, wrote a book of African tales. For many long years, it was not safe for them to return to Ghana.

Ira, Patient Farmer

With a tired sigh, Ira Johns walked in the back door of his two-story farmhouse in Elkhart County, Indiana. His face was grim as he hung his hat on the peg by the door.

Mrs. Johns, on her way from the stove to the kitchen table, said cheerily, "Oh, good, here you are! Supper's just ready." She glanced over at her husband, and noticed the look on his face.

"Ira, what's the matter?" she asked.

"It's the cows, Lizzie," he replied. "They're all getting sick now."

"All of them?" she asked, her face creasing with worry.

"Yes. I tried to keep that new cow from spreading her sickness," Ira said. "But I guess it was just too late."

By now the Johns' eight children were gathering around the table to eat.

Ira turned away and silently began washing up at the basin. But the children had heard what their father said.

After prayers were said and supper begun, they started to ask questions.

"What's wrong with the cows?" asked little Galen, who was too young to help in the barn. All eyes turned to Father.

"They have something called Bang's disease," answered Ira in a serious voice. "Some people call it undulant fever. It makes cows very sick, and it spreads easily to other cows."

"How did our cows get it?" asked ten-year-old Pauline, flicking one of her braids behind her shoulder.

"Well, I guess it came from that new cow I bought from Mr. Yoder," said her father. "I didn't know she was sick when I got her, but soon she got real weak and was shivering with chills. I tried to keep her away from the other cows, but it was too late. They're all coming down with it now."

Ira looked so tired and concerned that the children didn't know what to say. Most of them stared down at their plates and pretended to eat. Finally Daniel, the oldest boy, asked, "Didn't Mr. Yoder know his cow was sick when he sold it to you? I thought cows have to be tested before they're sold."

"Well, yes, that's right," said Ira slowly. "I guess Mr. Yoder knew it, or else he didn't have the cow tested."

"That's not fair!" Daniel said, angrily. "He should give you your money back, *and* pay for all our sick cows!"

"Well, Daniel," his father said. "Mr. Yoder might not have the

money to pay us back. I certainly will tell him about it."

The next morning Ira paid a visit to Mr. Yoder and told him about the sickness that had spread from his cow to the Johns' whole herd. Mr. Yoder said he was very sorry and promised to make things right. Ira returned home, satisfied.

But days and weeks went by, and the Johns family heard nothing from Mr. Yoder. For months they could not sell cream from their cows because of the fever. If people used cream from infected cows, they would get sick too. So no cream could be sold until the cows were completely well.

It was hard for some people to understand why Ira Johns didn't hire a lawyer and force Mr. Yoder to pay him. But Ira wasn't only a farmer—he was a Christian and a preacher. He knew that Jesus wants his followers to forgive, and he did his best to live that way.

Every now and then, Ira would see Mr. Yoder and remind him of his promise. But no money ever came.

Many, many years went by. The Johns children grew up and married. They had their own children. In 1956 Grandpa Ira Johns died, without receiving a penny from Mr. Yoder.

Many more years went by, and the family gradually forgot all about Mr. Yoder and the sick cow.

One day in 1972, Galen Johns, Ira's youngest child, went to his mailbox and found a letter from a lawyer in a faraway state. When he opened it, he was surprised to find a check for more than two thousand dollars! It was from Mr. Yoder, who had recently died.

Before he died, Mr. Yoder had written in his will that $2,224.34 should be paid to the Johns family for the debt he owed them. Finally Mr. Yoder had kept his promise, almost fifty years after Ira had bought the cow from him!

The money was divided equally among the eight children of Ira and Elizabeth Johns. They were glad to remember the story of the sick cow and to tell their children about the patience and love of their Grandpa Ira, a follower of Jesus.

Loren Johns, son of Galen and grandson of Ira, shared this story with his church family one Sunday morning. It is a story that will continue to challenge generations of the Johns family.

Glenn, the Pitcher

The late summer day had been sunny and humid. Even
now, in the evening, the ballpark in Scottdale was dusty
and hot.

Two church softball teams were near the end of a close
game. Pitcher Glenn stopped a moment to mop his grimy
forehead. *I sure could use a cold drink*, he thought. *But the
game'll soon be over. It would be great to win this
championship game!*

It was the last inning. Glenn's team had already been at bat. The score was tied. The other team needed only one run to win. Working together, Glenn's team had gotten one, then two players out.

Just one more to go, thought Glenn, as he planned his next pitch. He wound up and threw a beautiful curve ball, but the batter managed to hit it with the tip of his bat. The ball spun crazily over to first, bouncing away from the first baseman, and the runner was safe.

Now the other team had a chance to score a run!

The next batter was a good one, Glenn knew. But he wasn't worried. Two times before that evening he had struck this player out.

It wasn't so easy this time. Glenn pitched hard, but soon the count was two strikes, three balls. Glenn had to be careful now, or the batter might walk to first base. He threw a fast ball.

CRACK! The batter slammed the ball straight back at Glenn, just over his head and out to center field. The center fielder charged in and caught the ball on the first bounce.

He hurled it over Glenn's head to the catcher at home plate. The first runner, who had been on second base, was already heading home. Nearing home plate, he began to slide. As he slid, the ball reached the catcher's glove.

"OUT!" yelled the umpire, as dust clouds rose above home plate.

Glenn's first feeling was relief. "Hooray! We got him out!"

But now a cry went up from the other team's bench. "No, he's safe! The catcher dropped the ball!"

Angry players leaped up and ran over to argue with the umpire. Glenn's team argued the other way. "He's out, you said! You can't change it now!"

In the middle of all the noise and confusion, Glenn stopped to think. He had seen the whole thing: The catcher caught the ball; then, as the runner slid in home, the catcher dropped the ball and quickly scooped it up again.

The other team was right! The catcher had dropped the ball. He did not have the ball in his glove when the runner reached home plate. So there was no out!

What shall I do? thought Glenn. *Should I say something? The safest thing to do is keep my mouth shut. I don't want my teammates mad at me. After all, it's the umpire's job to decide, not mine,* he told himself. But then he looked around at the players' angry faces and listened to their loud voices and accusing words. They were acting like they hated each other.

What would Jesus do? The answer was clear. From the time he was small, Glenn had learned that God loved the truth, that God had sent Jesus to bring peace and good will to people. Jesus wanted his followers to do that, too.

Slowly Glenn walked up to the umpire and stopped. He looked him in the eye and said, "The other team is right. I saw our catcher drop the ball."

The arguing and the noise stopped. Everyone stared at Glenn in shocked silence. His teammates couldn't believe their ears! Why was Glenn ruining their chance to be champions?

The umpire saw that he must have made a mistake. He called the runner safe, giving the win and the championship to the other team.

As for Glenn, he felt good inside. He knew he had done the right thing. After they had time to cool off, his teammates realized it, too. The hot and dusty summer evening in the ballpark ended peacefully after all.

Glenn Millslagle, Scottdale, Pennsylvania, inherited his ball-playing ability from his grandpa, who was paid to play on coal company teams. His experience in the ballpark that evening helped him to know that "being honest and peaceable is the best way to live."

Bishop Benedict

Young David Yoder leaned
forward in his chair at the
dinner table. Papa had heard
exciting news that morning, and
the family was all ears.

"Whose horse was stolen?" asked
Mama, dishing up more noodles
from the pot.

"Benedict Miller's," Papa answered.
"His finest one, too."

"Not the gray Percheron!" exclaimed
David. He thought sadly of the beautiful,
dappled work horse—huge, but gentle as a
lamb. That horse was the best in all of Somerset County! Who
would dare steal him? David began to feel angry instead of sad.

"Will they catch the thief?" questioned Mama.

"I don't know," answered Papa. "Hours have passed already.
The horse was probably taken in the middle of the night.

Benedict did find tracks of a man and horse going out the lane."

"That should help," said Mama. "Did he follow them?"

"No, that's the thing," said Papa. "Benedict refused to go after the thief. He said the Bible tells us not to demand the return of stolen goods."

"Well, that does sound like Benedict," Mama nodded.

She's right, David thought. Bishop Benedict Miller was the kindest man he had ever known. He was always taking strangers into his home and giving them work in his woodworking and blacksmith shops. He planted apple trees along the roadside so travelers could eat the fruit.

Best of all, Benedict had started a school in his home for David and the other Amish children. After all, he said, this was the 1830s and "die Kinder mussa lerna" (the children must learn).

David knew the kind bishop meant it when he said he would not go after his horse. Still, it was a shame that the beautiful Percheron was gone.

The community talked about it for weeks. Most of the people, especially the neighbors who weren't Amish, thought Benedict

should have followed the thief. But Benedict stood firm. He would follow Jesus' way—people were more important than property.

Months passed. The talk died down. Young David no longer thought about the gray Percheron every time he saw Bishop Miller. He no longer wondered sadly about the horse as he did his chores on the farm.

Then one day Papa came home with important news. A neighbor had seen a huge, dapple gray horse tied to a hitch rack in Baltimore, ninety miles away. He felt sure it was Benedict's horse.

"He talked to the owner," exclaimed Papa, "and the man said

he bought the horse a short time ago from a stranger! He agreed to sell the horse if we can prove it belongs to Benedict."

"Has the bishop been told?" asked Mama.

"Yes," answered Papa, "but he refuses to go claim the horse. We neighbors have decided to go together and buy the horse back for him. It just has to be Benedict's!"

A few days later an excited group of men and boys gathered on the road a mile from Benedict Miller's farm. Two men had led the huge, gray workhorse all the way back from Baltimore. Now he pawed the ground and snorted nervously as David's father began to remove his bridle.

Benedict had refused to take the horse back unless he returned on his own. David held his breath as the bridle dropped into his father's hands. What would the horse do? All eyes watched eagerly.

The huge gray Percheron shook his head and sniffed the air, enjoying his freedom. Then slowly he headed down the road toward Benedict's farm, walking proudly and easily. The men and boys followed, careful not to get too close.

As the horse reached Benedict's farm, he turned abruptly and walked down the lane toward the barn. When he entered the barnyard, Benedict, who had been waiting, called out his name.

But the great, gray horse ignored him and kept on walking. He walked through the barn door, into the stable, and into the first stall—his very own! Benedict Miller's finest horse had come home again, and the whole neighborhood rejoiced.

Benedict Miller, an Amish bishop in western Maryland and Pennsylvania, lived from 1781 to 1837. In all kinds of weather, summer and winter, he rode horseback to preach in scattered churches. This story about Benedict was taken from a collection put together by his descendants.

The Author

Mary Clemens Meyer grew up in the large family of a Mennonite pastor in Lansdale, Pennsylvania. Her fondest early memories include two-week Bible schools with an attendance of 350; hosting visiting preachers and missionary families; and the daily give-and-take of life with six older brothers and sisters, her parents, and a live-in grandmother.

Meyer graduated from Christopher Dock Mennonite High School in Lansdale, and from Goshen (Ind.) College, with a B.A. in art and communication. Besides writing, her interests include graphic and needlework design and fraktur painting.

She is writer of the nursery and preschool level of the Herald Press *Come and See Bible School Series* and co-writer of grade 5. She serves the Mennonite Publishing House as editor of *On the Line,* a weekly story paper for children ages ten to fourteen.

Meyer is mother of three young children, Susanna, Christopher, and Katie. Her husband, Ronald, is promotion manager for Provident Bookstores. The Meyers live in Scottdale, Pennsylvania, where they are members of Kingview Mennonite Church.